1001 COOL JOKES

with Glen Singleton

HB
HINKLER
BOOKS

Cover Design: Hinkler Books Studio
Cover Illustration & Illustrations: Glen Singleton

1001 Cool Jokes
Published in 2004 by Hinkler Books Pty Ltd
45-55 Fairchild Street
Heatherton VIC 3202 Australia
www.hinklerbooks.com

ISBN: 978 1 7412 1743 8
Printed and bound in China

CONTENTS

Animals	4
Dinosaurs	50
Miscellaneous	57
Monsters	80
Doctor Doctor	102
Food	117
Gross	128
Just Silly	132
Silly Inventions	142
Knock Knock	143
Riddles	174
Sport	187
Computers	191
What do you call	193
Silly Book Titles	196
Vehicles	204

Animals

1 **W**hat do you get when you cross an elephant with a fish?

Swimming trunks!

2 **W**hat happened when the dog went to the flea circus?

He stole the show!

3 **W**hat did the dog say when he was attacked by a tiger?

Nothing, dogs can't talk.

4 **H**ow did the skunk phone his mother?
On a smellular phone.

5 **W**hat do you get if you cross a cocker spaniel with a rooster and a poodle?

Cockerpoodledoo.

6 **W**hy are four-legged animals bad dancers?

Because they have two left feet.

7 **W**hat do you call a woodpecker with no beak?

A headbanger.

8 **W**hat do you get when you cross a mountain lion and a parrot?

I don't know, but when it talks, you had better listen!

9 **W**hat do you get when you cross a chicken and a caterpillar?

Drumsticks for everyone!

10 **W**hat do you call a lamb with a machine gun?

Lambo.

11 **W**hat do you get when you cross a high chair and a bird?

A stool pigeon.

12 **W**hat do cats put in soft drinks?

Mice cubes.

13 **W**hat's 150 feet long and jumps every ten seconds?

A dinosaur with the hiccups.

14 **W**hat do you call a camel with three humps?

Humphrey.

15 **W**hat do you call a penguin in the desert?

Lost.

16 **W**hat do you get if you sit under a cow?

A pat on the head.

17 **W**hat do you call a duck with fangs?

Count Quackula.

18 **W**hat did Mr. and Mrs. Chicken call their baby?

Egg.

19 **W**hat kind of tie do pigs wear?

A pigsty.

20 **W**hy don't turkeys get invited to dinner parties?

Because they use fowl language.

21 **W**hich side of the chicken has the most feathers?

The outside.

22 **W**hat did the duck say when she finished shopping?

Just put it on my bill.

23 **W**hat do frozen cows do?

They give ice cream.

24 **W**hat is a dog's favorite food?

Anything that is on your plate!

25 **W**hat did the hen say when she saw scrambled eggs?

What a crazy mixed up kid.

26 **W**hat do you get when you cross a rooster with a steer?

A cock and bull story.

27 **W**hy did the cow jump over the moon?

Because the farmer had cold hands.

28 **W**hy do mother kangaroos hate rainy days?

Because their kids have to play inside.

29 **W**hy did the chicken cross the basketball court?

He heard the referee calling fowls.

30 **W**hat do you call an elephant in a telephone booth?

Stuck.

31 **W**hat do you call an elephant that never washes?

A smellyphant.

32 **W**hat do you give a sick elephant?

A very big paper bag.

33 **W**hat's black and very noisy?

A crow with a drum set.

34 **W**hy do elephants live in the jungle?

Because they can't fit inside houses.

35 **W**hy are elephants wrinkled all over?

Because they can't fit on an ironing board.

36 **W**hy are skunks always arguing?

Because they like to make a big stink!

37 **W**hat do you call a cow riding a skateboard?

A cow-tastrophe about to happen.

38 **W**hat do you get if you cross a parrot with a shark?

An animal that talks your head off!

39 **W**hy did the elephant paint the bottom of his feet yellow?

So he could hide upside down in custard.

40 **D**id you ever find an elephant in custard?

No.

It must work then!

41 **W**hat's black and white and eats like a horse?

A zebra.

42 **W**hat do you get if you cross a centipede with a parrot?

A walkie-talkie.

43 **W**hat did the snail say when he hitched a ride on the turtle's back?

Weeeeeeeeeeeeeeeeeeeeeeee!!!!

44 **W**hat do you get if you cross a duck with a rooster?

A bird that wakes you up at the quack of dawn!

45 **D**id you hear the one about the dog running ten miles to retrieve a stick?

It was too far-fetched.

46 **W**hat's black and white and black and white and black and white?

A penguin rolling down a hill!

47 **W**hat do dogs and trees have in common?

Bark!

48 **W**hat is white, fluffy and lives in the jungle?

A meringue-utan!

49 **W**hat's bright orange and sounds like a parrot?

A carrot!

50 What's tall, hairy, lives in the Himalayas and does 500 sit-ups a day?

The abdominal snowman!

51 What is a slug?

A snail with a housing problem.

52 What do you get if you cross a skunk with a bear?

Winnie the Poo.

53 What's the difference between an elephant and a flea?

An elephant can have fleas but a flea can't have elephants.

54 Did you know it takes three sheep to make a sweater?

Hmmm. I didn't even know they could knit.

55 **W**hat would you do if a bull charged you?
Pay him cash.

56 **W**hat steps would you take if a bull chased you?
Big ones.

57 **W**hat happened to
the dog that
swallowed the watch?
He got ticks.

58 **W**hy is the sky so high?
So birds won't bump their heads.

59 **W**hy do giraffes have long necks?

Because their feet stink.

60 **W**hat's striped and goes around and around?

A zebra on a merry-go-round.

61 **W**here do bees go when they're sick?

To the waspital!

62 **H**ow do you milk a mouse?

You can't, the bucket won't fit underneath!

63 **W**hat time is it when you see a crocodile?

Time to run.

64 **W**hat time is it when an elephant sits on your fence?
Time to get a new fence.

65 **W**hat shouldn't you do when you meet a shark?
Go to pieces.

66 **W**hat do you call a baby whale?
A little squirt.

67 **W**hat are feathers good for?
Birds.

68 **W**hat do you get if you run a sparrow over with a lawn mower?
Shredded tweet.

69 **W**hat animal drops from the clouds?

A raindeer.

70 **A**re you a vegetarian because you love animals?

No, because I don't like plants.

71 **W**hy did they cross a homing pigeon with a parrot?

So if it got lost it could ask for directions.

72 **W**hat has four legs and goes "Boo"?

A cow with a cold.

73 **W**hat do you call fourteen rabbits hopping backwards?

A receding hareline.

74 **W**hy do gorillas have big nostrils?

Because they have big fingers.

75 **W**hat do you call a fly with no wings?

A walk.

76 **W**hat do you get if you cross a chicken with a yo-yo?

A bird that lays the same egg three times!

77 **W**hen is it bad luck to see a black cat?

When you're a mouse.

78 **W**hat's black and white and goes around and around?

A penguin caught in a revolving door.

79 **W**hy are
elephants gray?

*So you can tell
them apart from
canaries.*

80 **W**hat do leopards say after lunch?

"That sure hit the spots!"

81 **W**hat did the canary
say when she laid a
square egg?

Ouch!

Better move
to the
otherside
of the
street

82 **W**hy did the dog
cross the street?

*To slobber on the
other side.*

83 **W**hat's the difference between a barking dog and an umbrella?

You can shut the umbrella up.

84 **W**hy are dogs like hamburgers?

They're both sold by the pound.

85 **W**hat did the duck say to the comedian after the show?

You really quacked me up!

86 **W**hy do birds fly south?

It's too far to walk!

87 **W**hat do you give a pig with a rash?

Oinkment!

88 Ten cats were on a boat, one jumped off, how many were left?

None, they were all copycats!

89 Why did the chicken cross the road?

To see the man laying bricks.

90 What's black and white and makes a terrible noise?

A penguin playing the bagpipes.

91 What's a pelican's favorite dish?

Anything that fits the bill.

92 **W**hat do you get when you cross an elephant with a sparrow?

Broken telephone poles everywhere.

93 **W**hat did Thomas Edison Elephant invent?

The electric peanut.

94 **W**ho went into the tiger's lair and came out alive?

The tiger.

95 **H**ow do you start a flea race?

One, Two, Flea, Go!

96 **W**hat do frogs order in restaurants?

French Flies!

97 **W**hy does a hummingbird hum?

It doesn't know the words!

98 **D**id you put the cat out?

I didn't know it was on fire!

99 **H**ow do you know that carrots are good for your eyesight?

Have you ever seen a rabbit wearing glasses?

The rabbit who wouldn't eat his carrots as a child...

100 **W**hat does a crab use to call someone?

A shellular phone!

a romantic table for two in the corner next to the large rock amongst the coral

101   **W**hat has four legs and sees just as well from both ends?

A horse with his eyes closed.

102   **W**hat do you call a sleeping bull?

A bulldozer!

103   **W**hat do you get when you cross a cat with a lemon?

A sour puss!

104   **W**hat kind of cat shouldn't you play cards with?

A cheetah!

105 **H**ickory dickory dock,

Three mice ran up the clock,

The clock struck one,

But the other two got away with minor injuries.

106 **W**hat do you give a dog with a fever?

Mustard, it's the best thing for a hot dog!

107 **W**hy do cows wear bells?

Because their horns don't work!

108 **W**hat is gray, has big ears and a trunk?

A mouse going on vacation!

109 **W**hat did the porcupine say to the cactus?

Are you my mother?

110 **W**hat happened to the snake with a cold?

She adder viper nose.

111 **H**ow can you stop moles digging up your garden?

Hide the shovel.

112 **W**hat's the difference between a unicorn and a lettuce?

One is a funny beast and the other a bunny feast.

113 **W**hat would you get if you crossed a chicken with a mild-mannered reporter?

Cluck Kent.

114 **W**hat did Tarzan say when he saw the elephants coming over the hill?

Here come the elephants over the hill.

115 **W**hat is brown, has a hump, and lives in the North Pole?

A very lost camel!

116 **W**hat do you call a group of boring, spotted dogs?

101 Dull-matians!

117 **W**hy can't a leopard hide?

Because he's always spotted!

118 **W**hat did scientists say when they found bones on the moon?

The cow didn't make it!

119 **W**hat cat has eight legs?

An octopus.

120 **W**hat kind of dog tells time?

A watch dog!

121 **H**ow do you stop a rhino from charging?

Take away its credit card!

122 **W**hat do you call a pony with a sore throat?

A little horse!

123 **W**hat's the difference between a piano and a fish?

You can tune a piano, but you can't tuna fish!

124 **W**hat do you do with a blue whale?

Try to cheer him up!

125 **W**here do sheep go to get haircuts?

To the Baa Baa shop!

126 **W**hat looks like half a cat?

The other half!

127 **W**hy can't an elephant ride a tricycle?

Because they don't have thumbs to ring the bell!

128 **H**ow do you fit an elephant into a matchbox?

Take out the matches!

129 **H**ow do you fit a tiger into a matchbox?

Take out the elephant!

130 **W**hat is gray with sixteen wheels?

An elephant on roller skates!

131   **D**id you know that elephants never forget?

What do they have to remember!

132   **W**hy is a snail stronger than an elephant?

A snail carries its house, and an elephant only carries his trunk!

133   **W**hy is an elephant large, gray, and wrinkled?

Because if it was small, white, and smooth it would be an aspirin!

134   **W**hat did one firefly say to the other before he left?

Bye! I'm glowing now!

135   **W**hy was the father centipede so upset?

All of the kids needed new shoes!

136 **W**hat do
you call a
mad flea?
A looney-tic!

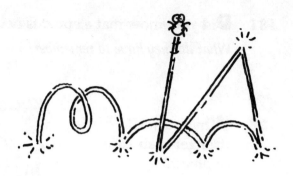

137 **W**hat kinds of bees fight?
Rumble Bees!

138 **W**hat are a bee's favorite soap operas?
The Bold & The Bee-utiful and Days of our Hives!

139 **W**hy was the bee's hair sticky?
Because he used a honey-comb!

140 **W**hy did the snail paint an S on its car?
So people would say "Look at that S car go!"

141 **W**hat do you call two spiders who just got married?

Newlywebs!

142 **I**f a snake and an undertaker got married, what would they put on their towels?

Hiss and Hearse!

143 **N**ame six things smaller than an ant's mouth?

Six of its teeth!

144 **H**ow do bees travel?

They take the buzz!

145 **H**ow do you make a snake cry?

Take away its rattle!

146 **W**hy did the firefly get bad grades in school?

He wasn't very bright!

147 **W**hat's worse than finding a worm in your apple?

Finding half a worm!

148 **W**here do you put a noisy dog?

In a barking lot!

149 **W**hat did the caterpillar say to the butterfly?

You'll never get me up in one of those things.

150 **W**hat do you call a fly
when it retires?

A flew.

151 **H**ow can you tell an elephant from a banana?

*Try to lift it up. If you can't, it's either an elephant or a
very heavy banana.*

152 **W**hat do you get when you cross an elephant with
peanut butter?

*Either an elephant that sticks to the roof of your mouth or
peanut butter that never forgets.*

153 **W**hat game do elephants play in a Volkswagen?

Squash!

154 **W**hat do
you call a monkey with a
banana in each ear?

Anything, he can't hear you.

155 **W**hy do tigers eat raw meat?

Because they can't cook.

156 **N**ow you see it, now you don't, now you see it, now you don't. What is it?

A black cat on a zebra crossing.

157 **W**hat is big, green, and has a trunk?

An unripe elephant.

158 **W**hat happened when the cow jumped over the barbed wire fence?

It was an udder catastrophe!

159 **W**hat do you call an unmarried female moth?

Myth.

160 **H**ow does an elephant get down from a tree?

He sits on a leaf and waits for autumn.

161 **W**hat do you get from nervous cows?

Milk shakes.

162 **W**hat do you get if you cross an alligator with a camera?

A snapshot.

163 **W**hy do elephants' tusks stick out?

Because their parents can't afford braces!

164 **W**hat's the biggest moth in the world?

A mam-moth.

165 **W**hat's the biggest mouse in the world?

A hippopotamouse.

166 **W**hat's green, wiggly, and goes "hith"?

A snake with a lisp.

167 **W**hy didn't the piglets listen to their father?

Because he was a boar.

168 **W**here can you buy ancient elephants?

At a mammoth sale.

169 **W**hy did the lion spit out the clown?

Because he tasted funny.

170 **W**hat did the beaver say to the tree?

It's been nice gnawing you.

NOW THAT'S A TASTY TREE!

171 **H**ow do you make toast in the jungle?
Put your bread under a gorilla.

172 **W**hat was the tortoise doing on the freeway?
About three miles an hour.

That's my funny bone!

173 **H**ow do you tell which end of a worm is the head?
Tickle him in the middle and watch where he smiles.

174 **W**hat do you give a sick bird?
Tweetment.

175 **H**ow do you stop an elephant from smelling?
Tie a knot in his trunk.

176 **W**hat has two
legs and two tails?

*A lizard flipping a
coin.*

177 **H**ow do you hire a horse?

Put four bricks under his feet.

178 **W**hat should you know
if you want to be a lion
tamer?

More than the lion.

179 **W**hy did the fly fly?

Because the spider spied her.

180 **W**hat's bright blue and very heavy?

An elephant holding its breath.

181 What did the
skunk say when
the wind changed
direction?

*Ahhh, it's all
coming back to me
now.*

182 Why did the viper vipe her nose?

Because the adder ad' er' ankerchief.

183 What's the best way to catch a rabbit?

Hide in the bushes and make a noise like lettuce.

184 What goes 99
bonk?

*A centipede with a
wooden leg.*

BONK

185 Why do
cows use the
doorbell?

*Because their
horns don't
work!*

DING
DONG

SQUEAK...SQUEAK...

HORNS
NOT
WORKING!

186 **W**hat's white on the outside, green on the inside, and hops?

A frog sandwich.

187 **W**hat does a porcupine have for lunch?

A hamburger with prickles.

188 **W**hat do you get when you cross a dog and a cat?

An animal that chases itself.

189 **H**ow can you tell a rabbit from a gorilla?

A rabbit looks nothing like a gorilla.

190 **W**hat did the goose say when he got cold?

"I have people-bumps!"

191 **W**hat lies down a hundred feet in the air?

A centipede.

192 **W**hat's the difference between a well dressed man and a tired dog?

The man wears a suit, the dog just pants.

193 **W**hat lives at the bottom of the sea with a six gun?

Billy the Squid.

194 **W**hat did the mosquito say when he saw a camel's hump?

Gee, did I do that?

195 **H**ow many skunks does it take to stink out a room?

A phew.

196 **H**ow do goldfish go into business?

They start on a small scale.

197 **W**hy do snakes have forked tongues?

Because they can't use chopsticks.

198 **H**ow do you spell "mouse trap" with three letters?

C A T.

199 **W**hat did the dog say when he sat on the sandpaper?

Rough, rough!

200 **W**hat is more fantastic than a talking dog?

A spelling bee!

201 **W**hat do you get if you cross a giraffe with a porcupine?

A 30-foot toothbrush.

202 **W**hat can go
as fast as a
race horse?

The jockey!

203 **I**f horses wear shoes, what
do camels wear?

Desert boots.

204 **W**hy don't kangaroos ride bicycles?

Because they don't have thumbs to ring the little bell.

205 **W**hat's the same size and shape as an elephant, but
weighs nothing?

*An elephant's
shadow.*

206 **W**hat's black,
white, and hides
in caves?

*A zebra who owes
money.*

207 **W**here do you find a no-legged dog?

Right where you left it.

208 **H**ow do you get an elephant up an acorn tree?

Sit him on an acorn and wait twenty years.

209 **W**hat did one flea say to the other?

Shall we walk or take the dog?

210 **W**hat did the cat have for breakfast?

Mice Krispies.

211 **W**hat goes tick tick woof?

A watchdog.

212 **W**hy was the chicken sick?

Because it had people pox.

213 **H**ow do you get down from an elephant?

You don't get down from an elephant, you get down from a duck.

214 **W**hat do elephants have that no other animal does?

Baby elephants.

215 **W**hat's big, white, furry, and found in outback Australia?

A very lost polar bear.

216 **W**hy do horses only wear shoes?

Because they would look silly with socks on.

217 **H**ow do you stop a pig from smelling?

Put a cork in his nose.

218 **W**hat's the difference between an African elephant and an Indian elephant?

About 3,700 miles.

Dinosaurs

219 **W**hat do you get if you cross a dinosaur with a vampire?

A blood shortage.

I vant to sark your blurd...

220 **W**hat do dinosaurs put on their french fries?

Tomatosaurus.

221 **W**hat's extinct and works in rodeos?

Bronco-saurus.

222 **W**hy did the dinosaur cross the road?
What road?

223 **W**hat do you call a
dinosaur with high
heels?
My-feet-are-saurus.

224 **W**hat do you get if you give a dinosaur a pogo
stick?
Big holes in your driveway.

225 **W**hat do you call a blind dinosaur?
Do-ya-think-he-saw-us?

226 **W**hat do you call a dinosaur that's a noisy sleeper?

Brontosnorus.

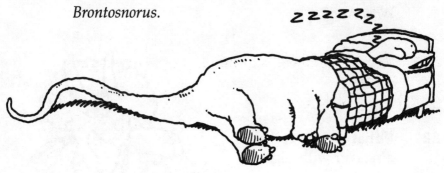

227 **W**hy did the baby dinosaur get arrested?

He took the bus home!

228 **W**hat's the best way to call a Tyrannosaurus Rex?

Long distance!

229 **W**hat does a Triceratops sit on?

Its Tricera-bottom!

230 **W**hat do dinosaurs put on their floors?

Rep-tiles.

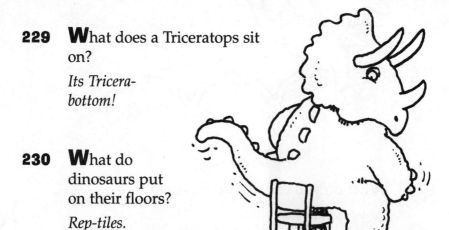

231 **W**hat dinosaur can't stay out in the rain?

Stegosaur-rust!

232 **W**hat do you call a group of people that dig for bones?

A skeleton crew.

233 **W**hat do you get when a dinosaur skydives?

A large hole.

234 **W**hat has a spiked tail, plates on its back, and sixteen wheels?

A stegosaurus on roller skates.

235 **W**hat's the difference between a dinosaur and a sandwich?

A sandwich doesn't weigh five tons.

236 **W**hat's worse than a Tyrannosaurus with a toothache?

A Diplodocus with a sore throat!

237 **W**hy couldn't the long-necked dinosaur see?

Because it had its head in the clouds!

238 **W**hat do you call a one-hundred million year old dinosaur?

A fossil.

239 **W**hat do you get if you cross a dinosaur with a dog?

A very nervous mailman.

240 **W**hat's the difference between dinosaurs and dragons?

Dinosaurs don't smoke

241 **W**hat did the egg say to the dinosaur?
You're egg-stinct

242 **W**hy didn't the dinosaur cross the road?
Because roads weren't invented

243 **W**hat do you call a scared tyrannosaurus?
A nervous rex

244 **W**hat dinosaur is home on the range?
Tyrannosaurus Tex

245 **W**hy don't more dinosaurs join the police force?
They can't hide behind billboards.

246 **W**hat do you call a
dinosaur eating a
taco?

Tyrannosaurus Mex

247 **W**hat do you call a dinosaur with magic powers?

Tyrannosaurus Hex

248 **W**hat do you call a dinosaur that destroys
everything in its path?

Tyrannosaurus Wrecks.

Miscellaneous

249   **W**hy is six scared of seven?

Because 7-8-9.

250   **W**hat did the egg say to the whisk?

I know when I'm beaten.

251   **W**hat is scared of
wolves and swears?

Little Rude Riding Hood.

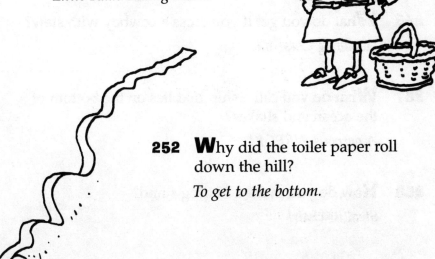

252   **W**hy did the toilet paper roll
down the hill?

To get to the bottom.

253 **W**hat's brown and sounds like a bell?
Dung.

254 **W**here are the Andes?

At the end of your armies.

255 **W**hat helps keep your teeth together?

Toothpaste.

256 **W**hat do you get if you cross a cowboy with stew?

Hopalong Casserole.

257 **W**hat do you call a ship that lies on the bottom of the ocean and shakes?

A nervous WRECK!

258 **H**ow do you make a hotdog stand?

Steal its chair!

259 **W**hy was Thomas Edison able to invent the light bulb?

Because he was very bright.

260 **W**hat's the best way to win a race?

Run faster than everyone else

261 **C**an a match box?

No but a tin can

262 **W**hy did the one-handed man cross the road?

He wanted to get to the second-hand shop!

263 **D**uring which battle was Lord Nelson killed?

His last one.

264 **W**hat did the floor say to the desk?

I can see your drawers.

265 **W**hy did the surfer stop surfing?

Because the sea weed.

266 **W**hat was more useful than the invention of the first telephone?

The second telephone.

267 **W**hat's small, annoying, and really ugly?

I don't know, but it comes when I call my sister's name.

268 **H**ow do you use an Egyptian doorbell?

Toot-and-come-in.

269 **W**hat side of an apple is the left side?

The side that hasn't been eaten.

270 **H**ow can you tell a dogwood tree?

By its bark.

271 **W**hat invention allows you to see through walls?

A window.

272 **W**hat are the four letters the dentist says when a patient visits him?

ICDK (I see decay)

273 **H**ow did the dentist become a brain surgeon?

His drill slipped.

274 **W**hat's another word for tears?

Glumdrops.

275 **W**hich months have 28 days?

All of them

276 **W**here does Tarzan buy his clothes?

At a jungle sale.

277 **H**ow do you make a fire with two sticks?

Make sure one of them is a match.

278 **W**hen do you put a frog in your sister's bed?

When you can't find a mouse.

279 **W**hy did Polly put the kettle on?

She didn't have anything else to wear.

280 **W**hat did the little light bulb say to its Mom?

I wuv you watts and watts.

281 **W**hy did the teacher wear dark glasses?

Because she had such a bright class.

282 **W**hy do toadstools grow so close together?

They don't need mushroom.

283 **W**hat did the judge say to the dentist?

Do you swear to pull the tooth, the whole tooth, and nothing but the tooth.

284 **W**hat happens when the Queen burps?

She issues a royal pardon.

285 **W**hat did one wall say to the other wall?

I'll meet you at the corner.

286 **W**here did the king keep his armies?

Up his sleevies.

287 **W**hy was the math book sad?

Because it had too many problems.

288 **W**hat's the letter that ends everything?

The letter G.

289 **W**hat did the stamp say to the envelope?

Stick with me, and we will go places.

290 **W**hat do you call a man with an elephant on his head?

Squashed.

291 **I** have ten legs, twenty arms, and fifty-four feet. What am I?

A liar.

You can say that again!

292 **W**hat did the tie say to the hat?

You go on ahead, I'll just hang around.

293 **W**hat do you call a boomerang that doesn't come back to you?

A stick.

294 **W**here was the Declaration of Independence signed?

At the bottom.

295 **W**hy does lightning shock people?

It doesn't know how to conduct itself.

296 **W**hat did the pencil sharpener say to the pencil?

Stop going in circles and get to the point!

297 What's the nearest thing to silver?

The Lone Ranger's bottom.

298 What do Alexander the Great and Kermit the Frog have in common?

The same middle name!

299 There are three kinds of people in the world. Those who can count. And those who can't.

300 What's the easiest way to get on TV?

Sit on it.

301 What has four legs and doesn't walk?

A table.

302 **W**here do you find giant snails?

At the ends of their fingers.

303 **N**ame three inventions that have helped man reach new heights.

The elevator, the ladder, and the airplane.

304 **W**hat's brown, hairy, and has no legs but walks?

Dad's socks.

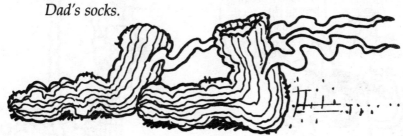

305 **H**ow do you saw the sea in half?

With a sea-saw.

306 **W**hat's easy to get into, but hard to get out of?

Trouble.

307 **M**om, why isn't my nose twelve inches long?

Because then it would be a foot.

308 **D**ad, can you see any change in me?

No, why son?

Because I swallowed twenty cents.

309 How did the rocket lose his job?

He was fired.

310 What's yellow and wears a mask?

The Lone Banana.

311 What has many rings but no fingers?

A telephone.

312 What do you get if you jump into the Red Sea?

Wet.

313 What's brown and sticky?

A stick.

314 What do you call a lazy toy?

An inaction figure.

315 **W**hy did the balloon burst?

Because it saw the soda pop!

316 **W**hat do all the Smiths in the telephone book have in common?

They all have telephones.

317 **W**hy do service stations always lock their bathrooms?

They are afraid someone might clean them.

318 **W**hat do you get if you cross the Atlantic with the Titanic?

About half way.

319 **W**hy did the bacteria cross the microscope?

To get to the other slide.

320 **W**hat do you do if your nose goes on strike?

Picket.

321 **W**hat's the hardest part about sky diving?

The ground!

322 **W**hat's the difference between a TV and a newspaper?

Ever tried swatting a fly with a TV?

323 **W**hat did the little mountain say to the big mountain?

Hi Cliff!

324 **W**hy did the traffic light turn red?

You would too if you had to change in the middle of the street!

325 **H**ow much does it cost for a pirate to get earrings?

A buccaneer!

326 **W**hat is the difference between a jeweller and a jailer?

A jeweller sells watches and a jailer watches cells!

327 **W**hat did the digital clock say to its mother?

Look ma, no hands.

328 **W**hy didn't the man die when he drank poison?

Because he was in the living room.

329 **W**hat do hippies do?

They hold your leggies on.

330 **W**hat did Snow White say while she waited for her photos?

Someday my prints will come!

331 **W**hat did one rain drop say to the other?

Two's company, three's a cloud.

332 **W**hat do you call a snowman with a suntan?

A puddle!

333 **W**hat did the penny say to the other penny?

We make perfect cents.

334 **W**hat did the Pacific Ocean say to the Atlantic Ocean?

Nothing. It just waved.

335 **W**ho was the smallest man in the world?

The guard that fell asleep on his watch.

336 **W**hat can jump higher than a house?

Anything, houses can't jump!

337 **W**hy did the bungy jumper take a vacation?

Because he was at the end of his rope.

338 **W**hy did E.T. have such big eyes?

Because he saw his phone bill.

339 **W**hat sort of star is dangerous?

A shooting star.

340 **W**hy did the belt go to jail?

Because it held up a pair of pants.

341 **W**hat is the name of the detective who sings quietly to himself while solving crimes?

Sherlock Hums!

342 **W**hy was the butcher worried?

His job was at steak!

343 **W**hat's the difference between an elephant and a matterbaby?

What's a matterbaby?

Nothing, but thanks for asking!

344 **W**hat did the shirt say to the blue jeans?

Meet you on the clothesline—that's where I hang out!

345 **W**hat did the big hand of the clock say to the little hand?

Got a minute?

346 **W**hat kind of music does your father like to sing?

Pop music.

347 **W**hat's the easiest way to find a pin in your carpet?

Walk around in your bare feet.

348 **W**hat did the parents say to their son who wanted to play drums?

Beat it!

349 **W**here do you find baby soldiers?

In the infantry.

350 **C**an February March?

No. But April May.

351 **W**hat's the definition of intense?

That's where campers sleep.

352 **W**hat do you call a man who stands around and makes faces all day?

A clockmaker.

353 **W**hat did one toilet say to the other toilet?

You look a bit flushed!

354 **D**id you hear the one about the man that went into the cloning shop?

When he came out he was beside himself!

355 **W**hat did the key say to the glue?

"You wanna be in show biz kid? Stick to me, I can open doors for you!"

356 **W**hen does B come after U?

When you take some of its honey!

357 **W**hy was the archaeologist upset?

His job was in ruins!

358 **W**here does a sick ship go?

To the dock.

359 **D**id I tell you the joke about the high wall?

I'd better not, you might not get over it.

360 **W**hat did the first mind reader say to the second mind reader?

You're all right, how am I?

361 **W**hat did one ear say to the other ear?

Between you and me we need a haircut.

362 **W**hat flowers grow under your nose?

Tulips.

363 **W**hat did the ear 'ear?

Only the nose knows.

364 **D**id you know that Davey Crockett had three ears?

A right ear, a left ear, and a wild frontier.

365 **W**hy does the ocean roar?

You would too if you had crabs on your bottom.

366 **W**hat will go up a drainpipe down, but won't go down a drainpipe up?

An umbrella

367 **W**hat would you call superman if he lost all his powers?

Man.

368 **W**hat has a hundred legs, but can't walk?

Fifty pairs of pants.

369 I have five noses, seven ears, and four mouths. What am I?

Very ugly.

370 What did one eye say to the other eye?

Something that smells has come between us.

Monsters

371 Little Monster: I hate my teacher's guts!

Mommy Monster: Then just eat around them!

You wouldn't like me if I start to cry...

372 Whats green, sits in the corner, and cries?

The Incredible Sulk.

373 What's a vampire's favorite dog?

A bloodhound!

374 What do vampires cross the sea in?

Blood vessels.

375 **W**hat did the alien say to the gas pump?

Take your finger out of your ear when I'm talking to you.

376 **W**hat did King Kong say when his sister had a baby?

Well I'll be a monkey's uncle.

377 **W**hy did the zombie decide to stay in his coffin?

He felt rotten.

378 **W**hat happened when the abominable snowman ate a curry?

He melted.

379 **W**hat do you call a good looking, kind, and considerate monster?

A complete failure.

380 Little Monster: Should I eat my fries with my fingers?

Mommy Monster: No, you should eat them separately!

381 Mom, everyone at school calls me a werewolf.

Ignore them and comb your face.

Remember... always part your face on the left dear...

382 What do sea monsters eat for lunch?

Potato ships!

383 Why did the cyclops give up teaching?

Because he only had one pupil.

I thought it had a couple more miles left in it yet ...

384 Why do witches fly on broomsticks?

Because it's better than walking.

385 **W**hy did Dracula take some medicine?

To stop his coffin.

386 **W**hat do devils drink?

Demonade.

387 **W**hat don't zombies wear on boat trips?

Life jackets.

388 **W**hat do you call a sleeping monster who won't keep quiet?

Frankensnore.

389 **W**hat happened to Frankenstein's monster when he was caught speeding?

He was fined $50 and dismantled for six months.

390 **H**ow does a monster count to thirteen?

On his fingers.

391 **W**hat happened to the monster that took the five o'clock train home?

He had to give it back.

392 **W**hat kind of cheese do monsters eat?

Monsterella!

393 **W**hat do you get when you cross a vampire and a snowman?

Frostbite!

Aww Mom I hate my B-Negative cold!

394 **M**other vampire to son:

Hurry up and eat your breakfast before it clots.

395 **W**hat do you call
a monster that
was locked in the
freezer overnight?

A cool ghoul!

396 **W**hat do you call
a single vampire?

A bat-chelor.

397 **W**hat did the witch say to the vampire?

Get a life

398 **W**hat do you get when you cross a skunk with
Frankenstein?

Stinkenstein!

399 **W**hat do you call a ten foot tall monster?

Shorty!

400 **W**hat is a vampire's favorite kind of coffee?

De-coffin-ated!

401 **H**ow can you tell a Martian would be a good gardener?

They all have green thumbs!

402 **W**hat does a monster say when introduced?

Pleased to eat you.

403 **W**hat did the baby zombie want for his birthday?

A deady bear

404 **W**hy did the sea monster eat five ships carrying potatoes?

Because you can't just eat one potato ship.

405 **W**hy doesn't anyone kiss vampires?

Because they have bat breath.

406 **W**hat do you think
the tiniest vampire
gets up to at night?
Your ankles.

Little
bloodsucka

407 **W**hy do ghosts go
to parties?
To have a wail of a time.

408 **W**hy aren't vampires welcome in blood banks?
Because they only make withdrawals.

409 **W**hy do ghosts hate
rain?
*It dampens their
spirits.*

410 **W**hat time is it
when a monster gets
into your bed?
Time to get a new bed!

411 **W**hy did they call the Cyclops a playboy?
Because he had an eye for the ladies!

412 **W**hat does a ghost have to get before he can scare
anyone?
A haunting license.

413 **W**hat did one ghost say to the other?

Don't spook until you're spooken to!

all I said was OOOOOooHHHH

414 **W**hat do you call a witch that lives at the beach?

A sand witch!

415 **H**ow do you make a witch scratch?

Take away the W!

416 **W**hy do mummies have trouble keeping friends?

They're too wrapped up in themselves.

417 **W**hat do you get when a ghost sits in a tree?

Petrified wood!

418 How many
witches does it
take to change a
light bulb?

*Just one, but she
changes it into a
toad!*

419 Who is the best dancer at a monster party?
The Boogie Man!

420 What is a monster's favorite drink?
Ghoul-Aid!

421 Where does a ghost go on Saturday nights?
Somewhere he can boogie!

422 **W**hat is a spook's favorite ride?

A roller-ghoster!

423 **W**hat is the difference between a huge smelly monster and candy?

People like candy!

424 **W**hat is Dracula's favorite fruit?
Necktarines!

425 **W**hat is Dracula's favorite place in New York?
The Vampire State Building!

426 **W**hat is a ghost's favorite dessert?
Boo-berries and I Scream!

427 **W**hy can't the Invisible Man pass school?

The teacher always marks him absent!

428 **W**hy did the monster eat the North Pole?

He was in the mood for a frozen dinner!

429 **W**hat is the best way to call Frankenstein's monster?

Long distance!

430 **W**hat is a ghost's favorite bedtime story?

Little Boo Peep!

431 **W**hat kind of mistake does a ghost make?

A boo-boo!

432 **W**hy do they have a fence around the graveyard?

Everyone is dying to get in!

433 **W**hat is big, hairy, and bounces up and down?

A monster on a pogo stick!

434 **W**hat is a ghost's favorite type of fruit?

Boo-berry!

435 **W**hat did the vampire say when he had bitten someone?

It's been nice gnawing you!

436 **W**hat did the skeleton say to the twin witches?

Which witch is which?

437 **W**hy is the vampire so unpopular?

Because he is a pain in the neck!

438 **W**hat does a ghost do when he gets in a car?
Puts his sheet belt on!

439 **W**hy didn't the ghost eat liver?
He didn't have the stomach for it!

440 **W**hat did the baby monster say to his babysitter?
I want my mummy!

441 **W**hat do you call five witches on a broom?
A broom pool!

442 **W**hy did Dr. Jekyll cross the road?
To get to the other Hyde!

443 **W**hat kind of fur do you get from a werewolf?

As fur away as you can get!

444 **W**ho did the monster take to the Halloween dance?

His ghoul friend!

445 **W**hy did Godzilla get a ticket?

He ran through a stomp sign!

446 **W**hat do you call a monster sleeping in a chandelier?

A light sleeper.

447 **W**hat is a mummy's favorite kind of music?

Rap!

448 **W**hat kind of boots do spooks wear?

Ghoulashes!

449 **W**here do ghosts live?

On dead ends!

450 **W**hy are ghosts such terrible liars?

Because you can see right through them.

451 **W**hat's a skeleton?

Someone with their outside off and their insides out.

452 **W**hat do you call a dumb skeleton?

A numbskull.

453 **W**hat kind of witch turns out the lights?

A Light-witch!

454 **W**hat did one skeleton say to the other?

If we had any guts, we'd get out of here!

455 **W**hat do you call a vampire's dog?

A Blood Hound!

456 **H**ow do you know when a ghost is sad?

He says Booooooooo Hoooooooo!

I hate those sad movies where the ghost gets exorcised

457 **W**hat do you do with a green monster?

Put him in a paper bag till he ripens.

458 **D**id you hear about the ghost who ate all the Christmas decorations?

He got tinselitis.

459 **W**hat do little ghosts play with?

Deady bears.

460 **W**hat is Dracula's favorite ice cream flavor?

Vein-illa!

461 **W**hy did the little monsters stay up all night?

They were studying for a blood test.

462 **W**hat do baby ghosts wear on their feet?

Booties!

463 **W**hy did the troll tell jokes to the mirror?

He wanted to see it crack up!

464 **W**hy do skeletons play the piano in church?

Because they don't have any organs!

465 **H**ow can you tell if a vampire has a cold?

He starts coffin!

466 **W**hat is a witch's favorite class in school?

Spelling!

467 **W**hat bear goes around scaring other animals?

Winnie The Boo!

468 **W**hat does a ghost read every day?

His horrorscope.

469 **W**here does Frankenstein's wife have her hair done?

At an ugly parlor.

470 **W**hat game do young ghosts love?

Hide and shriek.

471 **H**ow does an alien congratulate someone?

He gives him a high six.

472 **H**ow do monsters like their eggs?

Terrifried.

473 **W**hy couldn't the skeleton go to the dance?

He had no body to go with.

474 **W**hy didn't the skeleton cross the road?

Because he didn't have the guts to!

475 **W**hy did it take the monster ten months to finish a book?

Because he wasn't very hungry.

476 **H**ow many vampires does it take to change a light bulb?

None. They love the dark.

477 **W**hy are skeletons afraid of dogs?

Because dogs like bones.

478 **W**hat does a monster eat after he's been to the dentist?

The dentist.

479 **W**here do ghosts play golf?

At the golf corpse.

HA
HA
HA

480 **W**hat do you call the winner of a monster beauty contest?

Ugly.

481 **H**ow do you make a skeleton laugh?

Tickle his funnybone.

482 **W**hat do witches put in their hair?

Scare spray.

483 **W**hy are skeletons usually so calm?

Nothing gets under their skin!

484 **W**hat do ghosts eat for dinner?

Spook-etti

485 **W**hy don't skeletons wear shorts?

Because they have bony knees.

486 **D**o zombies have trouble getting dates?

No, they can usually dig someone up.

487 **W**hat does a boy monster do when a girl monster rolls her eyes at him?

He rolls them back to her.

488 **W**hat do you call a twenty ton two-headed monster?

Sir.

Doctor, Doctor,

489 **D**octor, Doctor, I have a hoarse throat.

The resemblance doesn't end there.

490 **D**octor, Doctor, what is the best way to avoid biting insects?

Don't bite any.

491 **D**octor, Doctor, I feel like a tennis racket.

You must be too highly strung.

492 **D**octor, Doctor, my nose is running.

You'd better tie it up then.

493 **D**octor, Doctor, I'm afraid of the dark.

Then leave the light on.

494 Doctor, Doctor, I keep stealing things.

Take one of these pills, and if that doesn't work, bring me back a computer.

495 Doctor, Doctor, I feel like a pair of socks.

Well I'll be darned.

496 Doctor, Doctor, I think I'm a video.

I thought I'd seen you before.

497 Doctor, Doctor I keep thinking I'm a yo-yo.

How are you feeling?
Oh, up and down.

498 Doctor, Doctor, how can I stop my nose from running?

Stick your foot out and trip it.

499 Doctor, Doctor, people keep disagreeing with me.

No they don't.

500 **D**octor, Doctor, I'm so ugly what can I do about it?

Hire yourself out for Halloween parties.

501 **D**octor, Doctor, I feel run down.

You should be more careful crossing the road then.

502 **D**octor, Doctor, I'm at death's door.

Don't worry, I'll pull you through.

503 **D**octor, Doctor, my stomach is sore.

Stop your belly aching.

504 **D**octor, doctor, I'm having trouble breathing.

I'll put a stop to that.

505 **W**hy do doctors wear masks?

Because if they make a mistake, the person won't know who did it!

506 **D**octor, Doctor I feel like a dog!

Then go see a vet!

507 **D**octor, Doctor, I keep thinking I'm a doorknob.

Now don't fly off the handle.

508 **D**octor, Doctor, I'm a wrestler and I feel awful.

Get a grip on yourself then.

509 **D**octor, Doctor, some days I feel like a tee-pee, and other days I feel like a wig-wam.

You're two tents.

510 **D**octor, Doctor, I keep thinking I'm a dog.

How long has this been going on?

Ever since I was a pup.

511 **D**octor, Doctor, everyone hates me.

Don't be silly, not everyone has met you yet.

512 **D**octor, Doctor, I'm suffering from hallucinations.

I'm sure you are only imagining it.

513 **D**octor, Doctor, I feel like a piano.

Wait a moment while I make some notes.

514 **D**octor, Doctor, will you treat me?

No, you'll have to pay like everybody else.

515 **D**octor, Doctor I keep thinking I'm a $10 bill.

Go shopping, the change will do you good

516 **D**octor, Doctor, I swallowed a spoon.

Well try to relax and don't stir.

517 **D**octor, Doctor, can you give me anything for excessive wind?

Sure, here's a kite.

518 **D**octor, Doctor, I swallowed a roll of film.

Don't worry, nothing will develop.

519 **D**octor, Doctor, I was playing a kazoo and I swallowed it.

Lucky you weren't playing the piano.

520 **D**octor, Doctor, nobody ever listens to me.

Next!

521 Doctor, Doctor, I keep thinking I'm a joke.

Don't make me laugh.

522 Doctor, Doctor, I'm turning into a trash can.

Don't talk such rubbish.

523 Doctor, Doctor, I feel like an apple.

Well don't worry, I won't bite.

524 Doctor, Doctor, I feel like a bell.

Well take these, and if they don't work, give me a ring.

525 Doctor, Doctor, I'm as sick as a dog.

Well I can't help you because I'm not a vet.

526 **D**octor, Doctor, my eyesight is getting worse.

You're absolutely right, this is a post office.

527 **D**octor, Doctor, the first thirty minutes I'm up every morning I feel dizzy, what should I do?

Get up half an hour later.

528 **D**octor, Doctor, what does this X-Ray of my head show?

Unfortunately nothing.

529 Doctor, Doctor, this ointment you gave me makes my arm smart!

Try putting some on your head.

530 Doctor, Doctor, something is preying on my mind!

Don't worry, it will probably starve to death.

531 Doctor, Doctor, I feel like a set of curtains.

Well pull yourself together.

532 Doctor, Doctor, I accidentally ate my pillow.

Don't be so down in the mouth.

533 Doctor, Doctor, I have a ringing in my ears!

Well answer it.

534 Doctor, Doctor, every time I stand up I see visions of Mickey Mouse and Pluto and every time I sit down I see Donald Duck!

How long have you been having these Disney spells?

535 Doctor, Doctor,
it hurts when I
do this!
Well don't do that.

536 Doctor, Doctor,
my leg hurts,
what can I do?
Limp.

537 Doctor, Doctor, I snore so loudly I wake myself up!
Doctor: Try sleeping in another room.

538 When do doctors get angry?
When they run out of patience (patients).

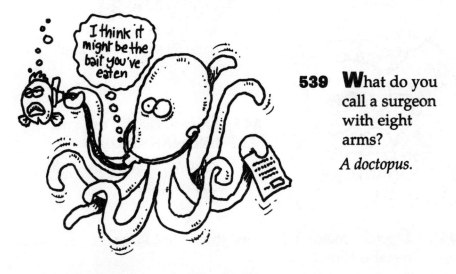

I think it might be the bait you've eaten

539 What do you
call a surgeon
with eight
arms?
A doctopus.

540 Why did the doctor tiptoe past the medicine
cabinet?
Because she didn't want to wake the sleeping pills!

541 Girl: Doctor, doctor everyone thinks I'm a liar.

Doctor: I don't believe you.

542 Doctor, Doctor, I feel like a pack of cards!

Sit down and I'll deal with you later!

543 Doctor, Doctor, I have a pain in the eye every time I drink hot chocolate!

Take the spoon out of your mug before you drink.

544 Doctor, Doctor, I only have 59 seconds to live!

Just a minute!

545 Doctor, Doctor, can you help me out?

Certainly—which way did you come in?

546 Doctor, Doctor, I dreamed that I ate a large marshmallow!

Did you wake up without a pillow?

547 Doctor, Doctor, I can't sleep at night!

Just lie on the end of your bed—you'll soon drop off.

548 **D**octor, Doctor—I'm invisible!

I'm sorry, sir, I can't see you right now.

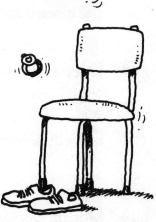

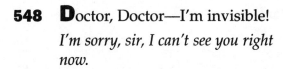

549 **D**octor, Doctor, my sister thinks she's a squirrel!

Sounds like a nut case to me.

550 **D**octor, Doctor, I think I'm getting shorter!

You'll just have to be a little patient.

551 **D**octor, Doctor . . . did you hear about the boy who swallowed a quarter?

No? Well, there's no change yet!

552 Doctor, Doctor . . . My son swallowed a pen, what should I do?

Use a pencil instead!

553 Doctor, Doctor, my wooden leg is giving me a lot of pain.

Why's that?

My wife keeps hitting me over the head with it!

554 Doctor, Doctor, my hair is falling out, can you give me something to keep it in?

Yes, a paper bag.

555 Doctor Doctor, I keep thinking I'm a billiard ball.

Well get back in the queue.

556 Doctor Doctor, I've been turned into a hare!

Stop rabbiting on about it.

557 Doctor Doctor, I keep thinking I'm a dog.

Well get up on this couch and I'll examine you.

I can't, I'm not allowed on the furniture.

558 Doctor, Doctor, can I have a second opinion?

Of course, come back tomorrow!

559 Doctor Doctor, I feel like a window.

Where's the pane?

560 Doctor Doctor will my measles be better by next Monday?

I don't want to make any rash promises.

561 What did one tonsil say to the other tonsil?

Get dressed up, the doctor is taking us out!

562 Doctor Doctor, I keep thinking I'm a fruitcake.

What's got into you?

Flour, raisins, and cherries.

563 Doctor Doctor, you've got to help me I keep thinking I'm a bridge.

What's come over you?

So far, a truck, a motorcycle, and two cars.

564 Doctor Doctor, I keep hearing a ringing in my ears.

Where else did you expect to hear it?

565 Doctor, Doctor, what's good for biting fingernails?

Very sharp teeth.

Food

566 **W**aiter, you've got your thumb on my steak!

Well I didn't want to drop it again.

If I don't it will slide off with everything else

567 **W**hy don't eggs tell jokes?

They'd crack each other up!

568 **W**hat did the banana sitting in the sun say to the other banana sitting in the sun?

I don't know about you, but I'm starting to peel.

Still peeling hey..? That sunblock really isn't working

569 **W**hat do you call a fake noodle?

An impasta.

570 **W**aiter, there's a fly in my soup!

Don't worry sir, the spider in your salad will get it!

571 **W**hat is a cannibal's favorite soup?

One with a lot of body.

572 **W**hat did the raspberry say to the other raspberry?

We shouldn't have got into this jam.

573 **W**aiter, what is this fly doing in my soup?

Freestyle I believe.

574 **H**ow do you fix a broken pizza?

With tomato paste.

575 **W**hat's yellow, brown, and hairy?

Cheese on toast dropped on the carpet

576 **W**hat stays hot in the fridge?

Mustard.

577 **H**ow can you tell the difference between a can of soup and a can of baked beans?

Read the label.

578 **W**hat has bread on both sides and is afraid of everything?

A chicken sandwich.

579 **W**hat nut is like a sneeze?

A cashew.

580 **H**ey! There's no chicken in this chicken pot pie.

Well do you expect to find dogs in dog biscuits?

581 **W**aiter, I'm in a hurry will my pizza be long?

No, it will be round.

582 **W**aiter, do you serve crabs in this restaurant?

Yes sir, we serve anyone.

583 **W**aiter, this soup tastes funny.

Why aren't you laughing then?

584 **W**aiter, this apple pie is squashed.

Well you told me to step on it because you were in a hurry.

585 **W**aiter, this egg is bad.

Well don't blame me, I only laid the table.

586 **W**aiter there is a small insect in my soup!

Sorry sir, I'll get you a bigger one!

587 **W**hy is a pea small and green?

If it was large and red, it would be a fire engine.

588 **W**here do bakers keep their dough?

In the bank.

589 **W**hy did the potato cry?

Because the chips were down.

590 **W**aiter, there's a bug in my soup.

Be quiet sir or everyone will want one.

591 **W**hy did the baby cookie cry?

Because his mother was a wafer so long.

592 **W**aiter, do you have frogs legs?

No, I've always walked like this.

The secret to making great wine...

dirty feet

593 **W**hat do you get when you step on a grape?

A little wine.

594 **W**hat did the teddy bear say when he was offered dessert?

No thanks, I'm stuffed!

NO!... not even a little mint

595 **H**ave you heard the joke about the butter?

I better not tell you, you might spread it.

596 **T**wo sausages are in a pan. One looks at the other and says, "Gosh, it's hot in here", and the other sausage says,

"GOODNESS GRACIOUS, IT'S A TALKING SAUSAGE!"

Ahhr stop griping and just sizzle away quietly like the rest of us

597 **M**om, can I have a dollar for the man who's crying in the park?

What's he crying about?

He's crying, "Hot dogs one dollar."

598 **W**hat's the difference between pea soup and roast chicken?

Anyone can roast chicken.

599 **J**ohnny, I think your dog likes me, he's been looking at me all night.

That's because you're eating out of his bowl.

600 **W**hat's long, green, and slowly turns red?

A cucumber holding its breath.

601 **W**hat do you make from baked beans and onions?

Tear gas.

602 **W**aiter, how long will my sausages be?

Oh about 3 inches.

603 **H**ow do you fix a cracked pumpkin?

With a pumpkin patch!

604 **W**aiter, there's a fly in my soup.

Yes sir, the hot water killed it.

605 **W**hy did the jelly wobble?

Because it saw the apple turnover.

606 **W**hat is red and goes up and down?

A tomato in an elevator!

607 **W**hy did the man at the orange juice factory lose his job?

He couldn't concentrate!

608 **H**ow do you make an elephant sandwich?

Well first you take an enormous loaf of bread . . .

609 **W**hy are cooks mean?

Because they beat the eggs and whip the cream!

610 **W**hy is a psychiatrist like a squirrel?

Because he's surrounded by nuts.

611 **W**hy should you never tell secrets in a grocery store?

Because the corn has ears, potatoes have eyes, and beanstalk.

612 **W**aiter, bring me something to eat and make it snappy?

How about an alligator sandwich, sir?

613 **W**hy did the cleaning woman quit?

Because grime doesn't pay.

614 **W**hy did the raisin go out with the prune?

Because he couldn't find a date.

615 **W**hy did Robin Hood rob the rich?

The poor didn't have any money.

616 **W**hat do you get if you cross a burglar with a cement mixer?

A hardened criminal.

617 **I**f I had six grapefruit in one hand and seven in the other what would I have?

Very big hands.

618 **H**ow do you make a sausage roll?

Push it down a hill.

619 **W**hat did the cannibal have for breakfast?

Baked beings.

There goes your Father again!

620 **W**hat did the baby corn say to the mother corn?

Where's pop corn?

621 **W**hat did one plate say to the other plate?

"Lunch is on me!"

622 **W**hy did the baker stop making doughnuts?

Because he was sick of the whole business.

Gross

623 **H**ow do you make a hankie dance?

Put some boogie into it.

Boy.... You've really got the boogie In you haven't you...

624 **W**hat is the soft stuff between sharks teeth?

Slow swimmers.

625 **M**ommy, Mommy can I lick the bowl?

No! You'll have to flush like everyone else.

Take that you filthy bad mannered brutes!!

626 **W**hy are sausages so bad mannered?

They spit in the frying pan.

627 **W**hy are basketball players never asked for dinner?

Because they're always dribbling!

628 **W**hat's the difference between a maggot and a cockroach?

Cockroaches crunch more when you eat them.

629 **W**hat's green, sticky, and smells like eucalyptus?

Koala vomit.

630 **W**hat do you get if you cross an elephant with a box of laxatives?

Out of the way.

Do you smell eucalyptus?

631 **W**hat is the difference between broccoli and boogers?

Kids don't like to eat broccoli!

632 **W**hy did Piglet look in the toilet?

He was looking for Pooh.

633 **W**hat do you find in a clean nose?

Fingerprints.

634 **W**hat's invisible and smells of carrots?

Bunny farts!!

635 **W**hat's the last thing that goes through a bug's mind when he hits a car windscreen?

His rear end.

636 **W**hy do little brothers chew with their mouths open?

Flies have got to live somewhere.

637 **H**ow do you keep flies out of the kitchen?

Put a pile of manure in the living room!

638 **W**hat's the difference between a worm and an apple?

Have you ever tried worm pie?

639 **H**ow can you tell when a moth farts?

He flies straight for a second.

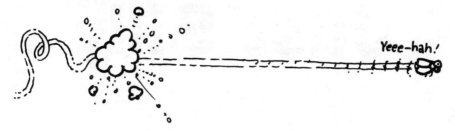

Yeee-hah!

640 **W**hat has two gray legs and two brown legs?

An elephant with diarrhea.

641 **W**hat makes you seasick?

Your little brother's vomit.

642 **W**hat is worse than finding a maggot in your apple?

Finding half a maggot!

643 **W**hat's another name for a snail?

A booger with a crash helmet.

644 **W**hat's yellow and smells of bananas?

Monkey vomit.

645 **W**hat's green, red, and goes at 70 mph?

A frog in a blender.

WORLD LAND SPEED RECORD
ATTEMPT

646 **W**hat has fifty legs and can't walk?

Half a centipede.

Just Silly

647 How do you know when a doofus has been making chocolate chip cookies?

There are M&M shells on the floor!

648 How did the doofus fall on the floor?

He tripped over the cordless phone!

649 Why did the doofus break into two windows?

One to go in and the other to go out.

650 What's that on your shoulder?

A birthmark.

How long have you had it?

651 What happened to the doofus that couldn't tell the difference between porridge and putty?

All his windows fell out.

652 What did the farmer say when he lost his tractor?

"Where's my tractor?"

653 Why did the doofus climb the glass wall?

To see what was on the other side!

654 **W**hy did the doofus get fired from the banana factory?

He threw out all the bent ones.

655 **W**hy was the doofus hitting his head against the wall?

Because it felt so good when he stopped!

656 **H**ow many fools does it take to screw in a light bulb?

three . . . one to hold the bulb, and two to turn the chair!

657 **H**ow do you confuse a doofus?

Put him in a round room and tell him to sit in the corner!

658 **H**ow do you get a one armed doofus out of a tree?

Wave to him.

659 **W**hat do you do if a doofus throws a hand grenade at you?

Pull the pin and throw it back.

660 **W**hat do you mean by telling everyone that I'm an idiot?

I'm sorry, I didn't know it was supposed to be a secret!

661 **H**ow can you tell when a doofus has been using the computer?

There is whiteout all over the screen!

662 **W**hat did the stupid burglar do when he saw a "WANTED" poster outside the police station?

He went in and applied for the job!

663 **H**ow do you keep a doofus in suspense?

I'll tell you tomorrow!

664 **H**ow did the doofus break his arm while raking leaves?

He fell out of the tree!

665 **W**hy did the doofus get fired from the M&M factory?

Because he threw away all the W's!

666 **W**hy did the doofus sleep under his car?

So he would wake up oily in the morning.

667 How do you sink a submarine full of fools?

Knock on the door.

668 Why was the fool's brain the size of a pea after exercising?

It swelled up!

669 What happened to the foolish tap dancer?

She fell in the sink.

670 Did you hear the one about the silly fox that got stuck in a trap?

She chewed off three legs and was still stuck.

671 **W**hy was the doofus covered in bruises?

He started to walk through a revolving door and then changed his mind!

672 **W**hat is the difference between a doofus and a shopping cart?

Shopping carts have a mind of their own.

673 **W**hy did the doofus go in the ditch?

Her turn signal was on.

674 Three tourists were driving down the highway trying to get to Disneyland. They saw a sign that read

'Disneyland Left.' So they went home.

675 **H**ow do you know if a doofus sent you a fax?

There's a stamp on it.

676 **D**id you hear about the doofus who did bird impressions?

He ate worms.

677 **W**hy did the doofus leap out the window?

To try his new jump suit.

678 **W**hy did the fool cross the road?

To get to the middle.

679 **W**hy did the fool put a chicken in a hot bath?

So she would lay hard-boiled eggs.

680 **H**ow do you make a doofus laugh on a Sunday?

Tell him a joke on Saturday.

681 **H**ow can you tell when there's a doofus on an oil rig?

He's the one throwing bread to the helicopters.

682 **W**hy did the doofus buy a chess set?
He was saving it for a brainy day.

683 **W**hat did the foolish ghost do?
Climbed over walls.

684 **W**hat happened to the stupid jellyfish?
It set.

685 **S**top! This is a one-way street?
Well, I'm only going one way!

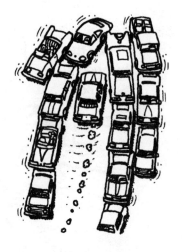

686 **D**id you hear about the doofus who paid five dollars to have his thoughts read?
He got his money back.

687 **W**hat did the doofus call his pet zebra?
Spot.

688 **D**id you hear about the doofus who got a boomerang for his birthday?

He spent the next two days trying to throw the old one away.

689 **D**id you hear about the bungee jumper who bounced up and down for 3 hours before they could bring him under control?

He had a yo-yo in his pocket!

690 **W**hat's red and hangs in an orange tree?

A silly strawberry.

Silly Inventions

691 **A**n ejector seat on a helicopter.

692 **A** parachute that opens on impact.

693 **W**aterproof teabags.

You know...I've used this tea bag over 250 times... I think the secret's in the plastic coating

694 **A** left-handed screwdriver

695 **A** one-way escalator

Knock Knock

696 **K**nock-Knock
Who's there?
Cargo
Cargo who?
Car go beep beep!

697 **K**nock-Knock
Who's there?
Alison
Alison who?
Alison to the
radio.

698 **K**nock-Knock
Who's there?
Police.
Police who?
Police let me in.

699 **K**nock knock

Who's there?

Gotter.

Gotter Who?

Gotter go to the toilet.

700 **K**nock-Knock

Who's there?

Mister

Mister who?

Mister last train home.

701 **K**nock-Knock

Who's there?

My panther

My panther who?

My panther falling down.

702 **K**nock-Knock

Who's there?

Aardvark

Aardvark who?

Aardvark a million miles for one of your smiles!

703 **K**nock-Knock

Who's there?

Caterpillar

Caterpillar who?

Cat-er-pillar of feline society

704 **K**nock-Knock

Who's there?

Norma Lee.

Norma Lee who?

Norma Lee I'd be at school, but I've got the day off.

705 **K**nock-Knock

Who's there?

Gladys.

Gladys who?

Gladys Saturday aren't you?

706 **K**nock-Knock

Who's there?

Witches.

Witches who?

Witches the
way home?

707 **K**nock-
Knock

Who's there?

Lettuce

Lettuce who?

Lett-uce in, it's cold outside.

708 **K**nock-Knock
Who's there?
Tank
Tank who?
You're welcome.

709 **K**nock-Knock
Who's there?
Turnip
Turnip who?
Turnip for school
tomorrow or there
will be trouble.

710 **K**nock-Knock
Who's there?
Sawyer
Sawyer who?
Sawyer lights on thought I'd drop by.

711 **K**nock-Knock
Who's there?
Freeze
Freeze who?
Freeze a jolly
good fellow.

712 Knock-Knock

Who's there?

Turnip

Turnip who?

Turn up the heater, it's cold in here!

713 Knock-Knock

Who's there?

Scott

Scott who?

Scott nothing to do with you.

714 Knock-Knock

Who's there?

Robin

Robin who?

Robin you! So hand over your cash.

715 **K**nock-Knock

Who's there?

Roach

Roach who?

Roach you a letter, but I didn't send it.

716 **K**nock-Knock

Who's there?

Nanna

Nanna who?

Nanna your business.

There are hundreds of perfectly good banks to rob... you great brute... ...so buzz off!

717 **K**nock-Knock

Who's there?

Harley

Harley who?

Harley ever see you anymore.

718 **K**nock-Knock

Who's there?

Luke

Luke who?

Luke through the peephole
and you'll see.

719 **K**nock-Knock

Who's there?

Boo

Boo who

What are you crying about.

720 **K**nock-Knock

Who's there?

Eiffel

Eiffel who?

Eiffel down.

721 **K**nock-Knock

Who's there?

Justin

Justin who?

Justin time for
lunch.

I'm on a diet for my weight....

722 **K**nock-Knock

Who's there?

Nobel

Nobel who?

No bell so I just knocked.

723 Knock-Knock
Who's there?
Minnie
Minnie who?
Minnie people would like to know.

724 Knock-Knock
Who's there?
Troy
Troy who?
Troy as I may, I can't reach the bell.

725 Knock-Knock
Who's there?
Kenya
Kenya who?
Kenya keep the noise down, some of us are trying to sleep.

726 Knock, knock.
Who's there?
Iran.
Iran who?
Iran 25 laps around the track and boy, am I tired!

727 **K**nock-Knock

Who's there?

Avon

Avon who?

Avon you to open the door.

728 **K**nock-Knock

Who's there?

Lionel.

Lionel who?

Lionel bite you if
you don't watch
out.

729 **K**nock-Knock

Who's there?

Cows

Cows who?

No, cows moo!

730 **K**nock-Knock

Who's there?

German border patrol

German border patrol who?

Ve vill ask ze questions.

731 **K**nock Knock

Who's there?

Ice cream!

Ice cream who?

Ice cream, you scream!

732 **K**nock Knock!

Who's there?

Pencil

Pencil who?

If you don't wear a belt, your PENCIL fall down!

733 **K**nock Knock

Who's there?

Tish

Tish who?

Bless you!!

734 **K**nock Knock

Who's there?

Shelby!

Shelby who?

Shelby comin' round the mountain when she comes!

735 **K**nock Knock

Who's there?

Dewayne!

Dewayne who?

Dewayne the bathtub before I dwown!

736 **K**nock Knock

Who's there?

Midas.

Midas who?

Midas well let me in.

737 Knock Knock

Who's there?

Euripedes.

Euripedes who?

Euripedes pants, Eumenides pants.

738 Knock Knock

Who's there?

Miniature.

Miniature who?

Miniature let me in, I'll tell you.

739 Knock Knock!

Who's there?

Arch!

Arch who?

Bless you!

740 Knock Knock!

Who's there?

Max

Max who?

Max, it doesn't matter who it is—just open the door!

741 Knock Knock!

Who's there?

Howard

Howard who?

Howard I know?

742 Knock Knock

Who's there?

Red!

Red who?

Knock Knock

Who's there?

Red!

Red who?

Knock Knock

Who's there?

Red!

Red who?

Knock Knock

Who's there?

Red!

Red who?

Knock Knock

Who's there?

Orange!

Orange who?

Orange you glad I
didn't say red?

743 Knock Knock!

Who's there?

Little old lady

Little old lady who?

I didn't know you
could yodel!

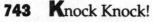

744 **K**nock Knock!
Who's there?
Artichokes
Artichokes who?
Artichokes when he
eats too fast!

745 **K**nock knock.
Who's there?
Letter.
Letter who?
Letter in or she'll
knock the door
down.

746 **K**nock knock.
Who's there?
Tuba.
Tuba who?
Tuba toothpaste.

747 **K**nock knock.
Who's there?
Phyllis.
Phyllis who?
Phyllis a glass of water
will you.

748 **K**nock knock.

Who's there?

Still.

Still who?

Still knocking.

749 **K**nock Knock!

Who's there?

Avenue

Avenue who?

Avenue heard these jokes before?

I'll come back again tomorrow... and the day after too

750 **K**nock Knock!

Who's there?

Wayne

Wayne who?

Wayne, wayne, go
away, come again
another day!

751 **K**nock Knock!

Who's there?

Debate!

Debate who?

Debate goes on de hook if you want to catch de fish!

752 KNOCK KNOCK

Who's There?

Ben

Ben who?

Ben knocking on the door all afternoon!

753 Knock knock

Who's there?

Ammonia.

Ammonia who?

Ammonia (I'm only a) little girl who can't reach the door bell!

754 Knock knock

Who's there?

Willube

Willube who?

Willube my valentine?

755 Knock knock

Who's there?

Water

Water who?

Water friends for!

756 Knock knock

Who's there?

William

William who?

William mind your own business?

757 **K**nock knock
Who's there?
Smore
Smore who?
Can I have smore marshmallows?

758 **K**nock knock
Who's there?
Arncha
Arncha who?
Arncha going to let me in? It's freezing out here!

759 **K**nock knock
Who's there?
M-2
M-2 who?
M-2 tired to knock!

760 **K**nock knock
Who's there?
The Sultan
The Sultan who?
The Sultan Pepper

761 **K**nock knock

Who's there?

Waiter

Waiter who?

Waiter minute while
I tie my shoe

762 **K**nock knock

Who's there?

Army

Army who?

Army and you still friends?

763 **K**nock knock

Who's there?

Wooden shoe

Wooden shoe who?

Wooden shoe like to know

764 **K**nock knock
Who's there?
Wednesday
Wednesday who?
Wednesday saints go marching in!

765 **K**nock-Knock
Who's there?
Jamaica.
Jamaica who?
Jamaica mistake.

766 **K**nock knock
Who's there?
Who.
Who who?
What are you—an owl?

767 **K**nock knock
Who's there?
Ice cream
soda
*Ice cream
soda who?*
Ice cream
soda
neighbors
wake up!

768 **K**nock knock
Who's there?
Shamp
Shamp who?
Why, do I have lice?

769 **K**nock knock
Who's there?
Empty
Empty who?
Empty V (MTV)

770 **K**nock knock
Who's there?
Vitamin
Vitamin who?
Vitam in for a party!

771 **K**nock knock
Who's there?
Despair
Despair who?
Despair tire is flat

772 **K**nock knock
Who's there?
Icon
Icon who?
Icon tell you another knock knock joke. Do you want me to?

773 **K**nock knock

Who's there?

House

House who?

House it going?

774 **K**nock knock

Who's there?

Closure

Closure who?

Closure mouth when you're eating!

WOW! These things REALLY DO WORK! I can see UNDERWEAR!!

X-RAY BINOCULARS

775 **K**nock knock

Who's there?

Icy

Icy who?

I see your underwear

776 **K**nock knock

Who's there?

Tick

Tick who?

Tick 'em up, I'm a tongue tied towboy

777 **K**nock, Knock.

Who's there?

Dishes

Dishes who?

Dishes a very bad joke..!!!!

778 **K**nock, Knock.

Who's there?

Weed

Weed who?

Weed better mow the lawn before it gets too long.

779 **K**nock, Knock.

Who's there?

Alaska.

Alaska who?

Alaska one more time . . . let me in!

780 **K**nock, knock.

Who's there?

Catch.

Catch who?

God bless you!

Would it be possible to have my SAMPLE LIPSTICK and my foot back please?

Door to Door COSMETICS

781 **K**nock, Knock.

Who's there?

Madam

Madam who?

Madam foot got stuck in the door

782 **K**nock, Knock.

Who's there?

Howdy!

Howdy who?

Howdy do that?

783 **K**nock, Knock.

Who's there?

Leaf

Leaf who?

Leaf me alone

784 **K**nock, Knock.

Who's there?

Butcher

Butcher who?

Butcher little arms
around me!

785 **K**nock Knock!

Who's there?

Stopwatch

Stopwatch who?

Stopwatch your doing and open this door!!

786 **K**nock Knock

Who's there?

Winner

Winner who?

Winner you gonna get this door fixed?

787 **K**nock, Knock.

Who's there?

Weirdo

Weirdo who?

Weirdo you think you're going?

788 **K**nock, Knock.

Who's there?

Canoe

Canoe who?

Canoe come out
to play?

789 **K**nock, Knock.

Who's there?

Radio

Radio Who?

Radio not, here I
come!

790 **K**nock, knock

Who's there?

Accordion.

Accordion who?

Accordion to the TV,
it's going to rain
tonight.

791 **K**nock, Knock.

Who's there?

Irish

Irish, who?

Irish I had a million dollars.

792 **K**nock, knock?

Who's there?

Alex.

Alex who?

Alexplain later, just let me in.

793 **K**nock, knock!

Who's there?

Zombies.

Zombies who?

Zombies make honey, zombies just buzz around.

794 **K**nock, knock!

Who's there?

Cameron.

Cameron who?

Cameron film are what you need to take pictures.

795 **K**nock knock.

Who's there?

Abbot.

Abbot who?

Abbot you don't know who this is!

796 **K**nock, knock.

Who's there?

Adore.

Adore who?

Adore is between us, open up!

797 **K**nock, knock.

Who's there?

Sombrero.

Sombrero who?

"Sombrero-ver
the rainbow . . . "

798 **K**nock, knock.

Who's there?

Alaska.

Alaska who?

Alaska no questions. You tella no lies.

799 **K**nock, knock.
Who's there ?
Irish stew.
Irish stew who?
Irish stew in the
name of the law.

800 **K**nock, knock.
Who's there?
Orson.
Orson who?
Orson cart!

801 **K**nock knock.
Who's there?
Felix.
Felix who?
Felix my ice cream, I'll
lick his.

802 **K**nock knock.
Who's there?
Cornflakes.
Cornflakes who?
I'll tell you tomorrow,
it's a cereal.

803 **K**nock knock.
Who's there?
Haywood, Hugh, and Harry.
Haywood, Hugh, and Harry who?
Haywood Hugh Harry up and open the door!

804 **K**nock knock.
Who's there?
Arthur.
Arthur who?
Arthur anymore jelly
beans in the jar?

805 **K**nock knock.
Who's there?
Theresa.
Theresa who?
Theresa green.

806 **K**nock knock.
Who's there?
Wilma.
Wilma who?
Wilma dinner be ready soon?

807 **K**nock knock.

Who's there?

Abbott!

Abbott who?

Abbott time you opened this door!

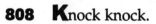

808 **K**nock knock.

Who's there?

Oscar

Oscar who?

Oscar silly question get a silly answer.

809 **K**nock knock.

Who's there?

Sancho.

Sancho who?

Sancho a letter, but you never answered.

810 **K**nock knock.

Who's there?

Celia.

Celia who?

Celia later alligator.

811 **K**nock knock.

Who's there?

Betty.

Betty who?

Betty late than never.

812 **K**nock knock.
Who's there?
Snow.
Snow who?
Snow good asking
me.

813 **K**nock knock.
Who's there?
Satin.
Satin who?
Who satin my
chair?

814 **K**nock knock.
Who's there?
Barbie.
Barbie who?
Barbie Q.

815 **K**nock-knock

Who's there?

Carrie.

Carrie who?

Carrie me inside, I'm exhausted.

816 **K**nock Knock!

Who's there?

Irish

Irish who?

Irish I knew some more knock, knock jokes.

Riddles

817 **W**hat are two things you cannot have for breakfast?

Lunch and dinner.

818 **W**hy did the boy throw butter out the window?

Because he wanted to see a butterfly!

819 **W**hat has eyes that can not see, a tongue that can not taste, and a soul that can not die?

A shoe.

820 **W**hat can you hear, but not see, and only speaks when it is spoken to?

An echo.

821 **W**hat is there more of the less you see?

Darkness.

822 **W**hat ten letter word starts with gas?
A-U-T-O-M-O-B-I-L-E.

823 **H**ow many apples can you put in an empty box?
One. After that it's not empty anymore.

824 **W**hen will water stop flowing downhill?
When it reaches the bottom.

825 **W**hat's black when clean and white when dirty?
A blackboard.

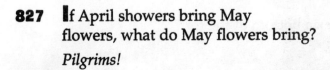

826 **W**hat's easier to give than receive?
Criticism.

827 **I**f April showers bring May flowers, what do May flowers bring?
Pilgrims!

828 **W**here can you
always find a
helping hand?

*At the end of your
arm.*

Can you give me a hand?

829 **W**hy do firemen
wear red
suspenders?

*To keep their pants
up.*

830 **W**hat kind of dress can never be worn?

Your address.

831 **W**hat weighs
more, a pound
of lead or a
pound of
feathers?

*They both weigh
the same.*

832 **W**hat word is always spelled incorrectly?
Incorrectly

833 **W**hat has a bottom at the top?
A leg.

834 **W**hy is milk the fastest thing in the world?

Because it's pasteurized before you see it.

835 **W**hat sort of ring is always square?

A boxing ring!

836 **W**hat's the last thing you take off before bed?

Your feet off the floor.

837 **W**hat starts with an "e", ends with an "e", and only has 1 letter in it?

An envelope!

838 **W**hat is always coming but never arrives?

Tomorrow.

839 **W**hat did the piece of wood say to the drill?

You bore me.

840 **W**hat can you serve, but never eat?

A volleyball.

841 **W**hat do you put in a barrel to make it lighter?

A hole.

842 **W**hat stays in the corner and travels all around the world?

A postage stamp

843 **W**hat do you call a bee that is always complaining?

A grumble bee!

844 **W**hat's taken before you get it?

Your picture.

845 **W**hich room has no door, no windows, no floor, and no roof?

A mushroom!

846 **W**hat gets wet the more you dry?

A towel!

847 **W**hat's green, has eight legs, and would kill you if it fell on you from out of a tree?

A pool table.

848 **W**hat washes up on very small beaches?

Microwaves!

849 **W**hat breaks when you say it?

Silence!

850 **W**hat gets bigger and bigger as you take more away from it?

A hole!

I can see CHINA..!!

851 **W**hat bow can't be tied?

A rainbow!

852 **W**hy are false teeth like stars?

They come out at night.

853 **W**hy do you go to bed?

Because the bed will not come to you.

854 **W**hat goes all around a pasture but never moves?

A fence!

855 **W**hat is H2O4?

Drinking!

856 **W**hat has teeth but cannot eat?

A comb!

857 **W**hat can you hold without touching?

Your breath.

858 What question can you never answer yes to?

Are you asleep?

859 What is the only true cure for dandruff?

Baldness!

860 What is big, red, and eats rocks?

A big red rock eater!

861 What goes all over the world but doesn't move?

The highway!

862 What starts with a P, ends with an E, and has a million letters in it?

Post Office!

863 What is always behind the times?

The back of a watch.

864 Why can't it rain for two days in a row?

Because there is a night in between.

865 **W**hat goes up and does not come down?

Your age!

866 **W**hat was the highest mountain before Mt. Everest was discovered?

Mt. Everest.

867 **W**hat goes up and down but never moves?

A flight of stairs.

868 **H**ow many seconds are there in a year?

12 . . . 2nd of January, 2nd of February . . . !

869 **W**hich candle burns longer, a red one, or a green one?

Neither, they both burn shorter!

870 **W**hat runs across the floor without legs?

Water.

871 **W**hich is the longest rope?

Europe!

GO EASY !!

872 **W**hat has holes and holds water?

A sponge

873 **W**hat puzzles make you angry?

Crossword puzzles.

874 **W**hat runs but doesn't get anywhere?
A refrigerator

875 **W**hat do you call a superb painting done by a rat?
A mouseterpiece!

876 **W**hat kind of ship never sinks?
Friendship!

877 **W**hat has four fingers and a thumb but is not a hand?
A glove!

878 **W**hat cup can you never drink out of?
A hiccup.

879 **W**hat kind of coat can you put on only when it's wet?
A coat of paint.

880 **W**hat belongs to you, but is used more by other people?
Your name.

881 **W**hat kind of cup can't hold water?
A cupcake.

882 **W**hat weapon was most feared by medieval knights?

A can opener.

883 **W**hen things go wrong what can you always count on?

Your fingers.

884 **W**hat flies around all day but never goes anywhere?

A flag.

885 **W**here were potatoes first found?

In the ground.

886 **W**hat can you give away, but also keep?

A cold.

887 **W**hat bet can never be won?

The alphabet.

888 **W**hat has two hands, no fingers, stands still, and runs?

A clock.

889 **W**hat is the beginning of eternity, the end of time, the beginning of every ending?

The letter "E".

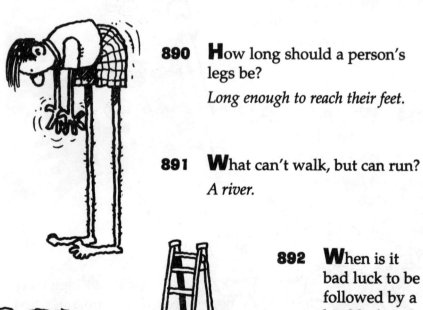

890 **H**ow long should a person's legs be?

Long enough to reach their feet.

891 **W**hat can't walk, but can run?

A river.

892 **W**hen is it bad luck to be followed by a big black cat?

When you are a little gray mouse.

Sport

893 **W**hy did the golfer wear two pairs of pants?

In case he got a hole in one.

894 **W**hat does every winner lose in a race?

Their breath.

895 **W**hy is a scrambled egg like the Bad News Bears?

They both get beaten.

896 **W**hat are the 4 seasons?

Baseball, basketball, soccer, & football!

897 **W**hat has 22 legs and two wings, but can't fly?

A soccer team.

898 **W**here do old bowling balls end up?

In the gutter!

899 **W**hat illness do martial artists get?

Kung Flu.

900 **W**hat position did the pile of wood play on the football team?

De-fence!

901 **W**hen is a baby like a basketball player?

When he dribbles.

902 **W**hy was the boxer known as Picasso?

Because he spent all his time on the canvas.

903 **W**hy did the runner wear rippled sole shoes?

To give the ants a fifty-fifty chance.

904 **W**hat did one bowling ball say to the other?

Don't stop me, I'm on a roll.

905 **W**hat's a ghost's favorite position in soccer?

Ghoul-keeper.

906 **W**hat happens when baseball players get old?

They go batty.

907 **W**hy were the arrows nervous?

Because they were all in a quiver.

908 **W**hat do you get when you cross a football player with a gorilla?

I don't know, but nobody tries to stop it from scoring.

909 **W**hy did all the bowling pins go down?

Because they were on strike.

910 **W**hy do soccer players have so much trouble eating?

They think they can't use their hands.

911 **W**hy was the centipede two hours late for the soccer match?

It took him two hours to put his shoes on.

912 **W**hy are basketball players always so cool?

Because of all the fans.

913 **W**hy was the chickens' soccer match a bad idea?

Because there were too many fowls.

914 **W**hy is tennis such a noisy game?

Because everyone raises a racket.

915 **W**hy is Cinderella so bad at sports?

Because she has a pumpkin for a coach, and she runs away from the ball.

Computers

916 **W**hy was the computer so tired when it got home?

Because . . . it had a hard drive!

917 **W**here are computers kept at school?

On their floppy desks.

918 **W**hat did the computer say when a man typed something in on the keyboard?

You're really pushing my buttons, little man!

919 **H**ow many programmers does it take to screw in a light bulb?

None, it's a hardware problem!

920 **W**here do you find the biggest spider?

In the world wide web.

921 **W**hy did the computer cross the road?

Because it was programmed by the chicken.

922 **W**hat do you get if you cross a computer programmer with an athlete?

A floppy diskus thrower.

923 **H**ey, did you see who stole my computer?

Yes, he went data way!

924 **W**hy did the computer sneeze?

It had a virus

925 **W**hat did the computer say to the programmer at lunchtime?

Can I have a byte?

926 **W**hat do computers do when they get hungry?

They eat chips

927 **W**hat is the computer's favorite dance?

Disk-o.

What do you call?...

928 . . . a man who likes to work out?

Jim!

929 . . . a girl with a tennis racket on her head?

Annette!

930 . . . a woman with a cat on her head?

Kitty!

931 . . . a woman with one leg?

Eileen!

932 . . . a boy hanging on the wall?

Art!

933 . . . a man with a map on his head?

Miles!

934 . . . a man with a car on his head?

Jack!

935 . . . a man who owes money?

Bill!

936 . . . a man with a spade?

Doug!

937 . . . a man without a spade?

Douglas!

938 . . . a girl with a frog on her head?

Lily!

939 . . . a man in a pile of leaves?

Russell!

940 . . . a woman in the distance?

Dot!

941 . . . a man with a Christmas tree on his head?

Noel.

942 . . . a woman with a Christmas tree on her head?

Carol.

943 . . . a lady standing in the middle of a tennis court?

Annette!

944 . . . a man with rabbits in his trousers?

Warren.

Silly Book Titles

945 "The Invisible Man" by Peter Out

946 "How to be Taller" by Stan Dupp

947 "A Terrible Nightmare" by Gladys Over.

948 "Famous Frights" by Terry Fied.

949   "Strong Winds" by Gail Forse.

950   "Swimming the English Channel" by Frances Neer.

951   "World Atlas" by Joe Graffie.

952   "Speaking French" by Lorna Lang Wedge.

953   "Close Shaves" by Ray Zerr.

954   "Great Eggspectations" by Charles Chickens.

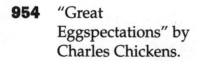

955   "How to be Shorter" by Neil Down

956 "Rice Growing" by Paddy Field.

957 "Horror Stories" by R. U. Scared.

958 "Up the Amazon" by P. Rhana.

959 "The Unknown Author" by Anne Onymous.

960 "The Long Walk to School" by Mr. Bus

961 "Infectious Diseases" by Willie Catchit

962 "Exercise At Home" by Ben Dan Stretch.

963 "A Bullfighter's Life" by Matt Adore.

964 "Broken Window" by Eva Brick

965 "The Mad Cat" by Claud Boddy.

966 "Egyptian Mummies" by M. Barmer.

967 "Hungry Dog" by Nora Bone

968 "A Hole in the Bucket" by Lee King

969 "Camping in Iceland" by I. C. Blast.

970 "The Poltergeist" by Eve L. Spirit

971 "A Ghost in the Attic" by Howie Wales

972 "Explosives for Beginners" by Dinah Might

973 "Ghosts and Ghouls" by Sue Pernatural

974 "The Omen" by B. Warned

975 "Famous People" by Hugh Did-Watt.

976   "Clairvoyance Made Easy" by I. C. Spooks

977   "Sahara Journey" by Rhoda Camel

978   "Jail Break" by Freida Prizner

979   "The Arctic Ocean" by I.C. Waters

980 "The Haunted House" by Hugo First.

981 "Stormy Day" by A. Pauline Weather

982 "Dealing With Bullies" by Howard U. Lykett.

983 "The Millionaire" by Iva Fortune.

984 "Easy Money" by Robin Banks.

985 "Roof Repairs" by Lee King.

986 "A Sting in the Tale" by B. Keeper.

987 "The Rainforest" by Teresa Green.

988 "Across the African Plains" by Ann T. Lope.

989 "Quick Snacks" by Roland Butter.

990 "Crossing Roads Safely" by Luke Bothways.

Vehicles

991 **W**hat happened to the wooden car with wooden wheels and a wooden engine?

It wooden go.

992 **W**hat did the traffic light say to the car?

Don't look now, I'm changing.

993 **W**hat flies and wobbles?

A jellycopter.

994 **W**hy can't a bicycle stand up?

Because it's two tired.

995 **W**hen is a car not a car?

When it turns into a garage.

996 **W**hat's a fjord?

A Norwegian car.

997 **W**hat do you give a sick car?

A fuel injection.

998 **H**ow can you find a lost train?

Follow its tracks.

999 **W**hat kind of car did Elvis drive?

A Rock-n-Rolls Royce.

1000 Policeman: Did you know that you were driving at 120 mph?

Driver: Impossible. I've only been in the car for five minutes.

1001 **W**hat do you call an expensive car with a cheap name?

A poor-sche.